KT-174-368

COUNTRIES OF THE WORLD

ITALY

SALLY GARRINGTON

Evans

TITLES IN THE COUNTRIES OF THE WORLD SERIES:
ARGENTINA • AUSTRALIA • BRAZIL • CANADA • CHILE
CHINA • EGYPT • FRANCE • GERMANY • INDIA • INDONESIA
ITALY • JAPAN • KENYA • MEXICO • NIGERIA • POLAND
RUSSIA • SOUTH KOREA • SPAIN • SWEDEN • UNITED KINGDOM
USA • VIETNAM

Published by Evans Brothers Limited
2A Portman Mansions
Chiltern Street
London W1U 6NR

VISIT OUR WEBSITE
Evans
www.evansbooks.co.uk

First published 2004
© copyright Evans Brothers 2004
Reprinted with revisions 2008

All rights reserved. No part of this publication may be
reproduced, stored in a retrieval system or transmitted
in any form, electronic, mechanical, photocopying,
recording or otherwise, without prior permission of
Evans Brothers Limited.

The right of Sally Garrington to be identified as the
author of this Work has been asserted by her in
accordance with the Copyright, Designs and Patents
Act 1988.

British Library Cataloguing in Publication Data
Garrington, Sally
Italy. – (Countries of the world)
1.Italy – Juvenile literature
I.Title
945

ISBN 978 0237 532888

Leabharlanna Dhún Laoghaire
J945

Produced for Evans Brothers Limited by
Monkey Puzzle Media Limited
Gissing's Farm, Fressingfield
Suffolk IP21 5SH, UK

Editor: Katie Orchard
Designer: Jane Hawkins
Map artwork by Peter Bull
Charts and graph artwork by Encompass Graphics Ltd
All photographs are by Edward Parker except *Camera
Press* 9 bottom; *Corbis Digital Stock* front endpapers, 6–7;
Still Pictures 44 bottom (Peter Frischmuth).

Endpapers (front): A view of the dramatic
Colosseum, in Rome.
Title page: Traders at the flower market in
Naples.
Imprint and Contents page: A row of gondolas
in Venice at dusk.
Endpapers (back): The unique mast sculpture
by artist Renzo Piano on Genoa's harbourfront.

CONTENTS

BAINTE DEN STOC

WITHDRAWN FROM DLR LIBRARIES STOCK

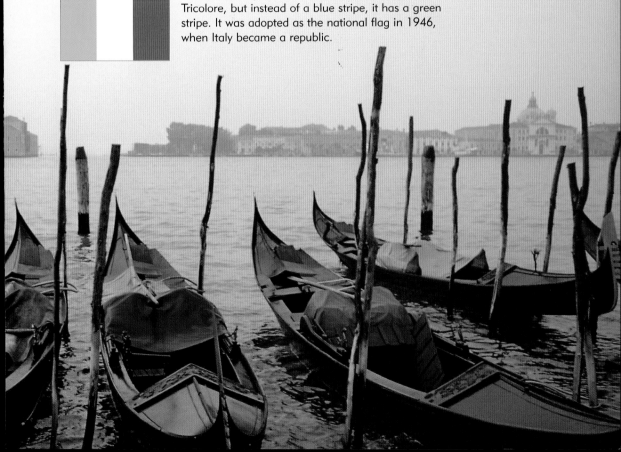

The Italian flag is based on the French flag, the Tricolore, but instead of a blue stripe, it has a green stripe. It was adopted as the national flag in 1946, when Italy became a republic.

A view of Rome seen from the Basilica of St Peter, showing St Peter's Square.

I taly as we know it today is a relatively young country – it was not unified until 1861. Within its 20 regions there is a rich diversity of culture, architecture and landscapes. Italy is also one of the most urbanised countries in Europe after the UK, Belgium and Germany.

Italy is located in southern Europe and has borders with Austria, Slovenia, Switzerland and France. Its northern regions are divided from the rest of the continent by the Alps. The boot-shaped peninsula juts out into the Mediterranean Sea. At its 'toe' is the island of Sicily, with the island of Sardinia further to the north and west.

Within the Republic of Italy there are two independent states: the Vatican, residence of the Pope and located within Rome; and the Republic of San Marino, Europe's smallest republic.

People sometimes refer to there being two Italies, one being the more industrialised and wealthy northern region centred around Milan. The other is the southern region, which is less developed, more dependent on agriculture and has a lower income per person, although this situation is changing.

A Colourful History

Although young as a united country, the land of Italy has a history stretching back over 3,000 years. The Roman Empire had a widespread influence in Europe and beyond. The Empire left behind a legacy of road and city building as well as engineering projects, including aqueducts. After the collapse of the Empire in AD 476, there were many invasions of peoples such as Germans and Muslim Arabs. In the twelfth century came the rise of the City States, when cities such as Venice, Florence and Genoa became independent and very powerful. Later on Italy was controlled by the Spanish, the Austrians and finally by the French, under the command of Napoleon. All of these influences have left their mark on the culture and architecture of the country.

In the nineteenth century, Garibaldi helped to create a unified and independent country. Since the Second World War, Italy has seen many changes of government, none of whom have managed to prevent the sense that Italy is still a country of two halves. Despite this division, the country has the world's eighth-

St Mark's Square in Venice is a major attraction for visitors to the city – and pigeons!

largest economy. In 1957, Italy became a founder member of the European Community, which later became the European Union (EU).

The Present Day

The Italians are a passionate and lively people with a great sense of style. The country itself has a rich cultural heritage and a broad range of natural landscapes. These factors continue to act as attractions for people both as a holiday destination and as a home.

Italian people have a reputation for fashion and design. Many of the world's top fashion houses are Italian.

KEY DATA

Official Name:	The Republic of Italy
Area:	301,300km²
Population:	58,147,733 (2007)
Main Cities:	Rome, Milan, Naples, Turin, Palermo, Genoa
GDP Per Capita (2006)*	US$30,200
Currency:	Euro (€)
Exchange Rate:	US$1 = €0.74
	£1 = €1.47

* Calculated on Purchasing Power Parity basis
Source: *CIA World Factbook*, 2007

Monte Bianco towers above the high Alps in the north-west of the country.

Italy is made up of a continental northern section and a relatively narrow peninsula section that juts out into the Mediterranean Sea. The peninsula divides the Mediterranean into the Tyrrhenian Sea to the west and the Adriatic Sea to the east. The country can be divided into five main landscape regions: the Alps, the Po-Venetia Plain, the Appennines, the coastal plains and the islands.

RELIEF MAP

GERMANY

LIECHTENSTEIN   A U S T R I A

SWITZERLAND

FRANCE

Monte Bianco (4,807m)

A L P S

Lake Como   Lake Maggiore

DOLOMITES

Val di Fiemme

SLOVENIA

Lake Garda

Adige   Venice

Ticino   Adda

CROATIA

Turin   Po

Po-Venetia Plain

SAN MARINO

BOSNIA - HERZEGOVINA

A D R I A T I C   S E A

Arno   •Florence

LIGURIAN SEA

Livorno

Tiber

A P P E N N I N E S

N

Elba

Corno Grande (2,912m)

CORSICA (FRANCE)

Rome

Ofanto

Naples ▲ Mt Vesuvius (1,218m)

Pontine Islands   Capri

SARDINIA

Val d'Agri

T Y R R H E N I A N

S E A

Cagliari

Stromboli ▲

Aeolian Islands   ▲Vulcano

M E D I T E R R A N E A N   S E A

Palermo •

SICILY   Mt Etna (3,323m)

Strait of Messina

| 0 | | 200km |
| 0 | | 100 miles |

THE ALPS

The Alps are fold mountains that connect the northern border of Italy with the rest of Europe. The highest point is Monte Bianco (Mont Blanc) at 4,807m, which rises on the French-Italian border. The eastern Alps are called the Dolomites.

Within the Alps there are many glaciers. The largest is the Miage Glacier on the slopes of Monte Bianco, which is 10km long. The sources of the Po, Ticino, Adige and Piave rivers are all on the south-facing slopes of the Alps. On the lower slopes of the Alps are large lakes, formed by the retreat of glaciers thousands of years ago. The three largest lakes are Lake Maggiore, Lake Como and Lake Garda.

Vegetation in the Alpine region changes according to altitude, with trees on the lower slopes, and alpine meadows and tundra high up in the mountains.

THE PO-VENETIA PLAIN

The Po-Venetia Plain is the largest lowland area in Italy. It follows the line of the Po Valley to the Adriatic coast, where the river has created a large delta over time. Other rivers, including the Adige and Tagliamento, have also helped build up the sediments of the delta. The large plain was once part of the Adriatic Sea. Today, the plain is densely populated. Little of the natural vegetation of willows, alders and oaks remains.

THE APPENNINES

The Appennine mountain range is often called the 'backbone of Italy'. For much of the peninsula the Appennines run parallel to the coast, but they are cut by valleys such as the Valle del Volturno in the south. Many rivers run east and west from these mountains, but they are much shorter than those flowing from the Alps. The highest peak in this region is the Corno Grande, in Gran Sasso d'Italia, at 2,912m. Much of this mountainous area has been deforested and overgrazed by sheep and goats. Heavy winter rains wash away the soil and reduce the fertility of the area.

COASTAL PLAINS

To the west and east of the Appennines are Italy's coastal plains. These are more extensive on the western side and run from Naples up to Livorno. The plain of the River Arno extends from the coast inland towards Florence. This large river plain is heavily populated. The plains around Naples are ideal for farming as they provide flat, fertile land with a warm Mediterranean climate.

THE ISLANDS

Italy has many islands, the two largest and most important are Sicily and Sardinia. The Appennines reach into northern Sicily and Mount Etna, a volcano, is located in the east of the island. The centre of Sicily is a large plateau. Sardinia has a mountainous interior with coastal plains, which are widest on the west coast.

Italy has many other small islands, mainly in the Tyrrhenian Sea. These include the Aeolian Islands, Capri, the Pontine Islands and Elba. Most of these islands rely on tourism as their main source of income.

The black sands on this beach on Stromboli show the island's volcanic origins.

VOLCANOES AND EARTHQUAKES

Italy has a major plate margin running through it, marking the boundary between two sections of the Earth's crust that are moving in different directions. The Adriatic Plate is part of the African Plate and is slowly moving northwards, whereas the Eurasian Plate is moving southwards. These movements often result in earthquakes. In the Alps earthquakes are sometimes felt as the two plates continue to collide and land is forced upwards. The Alps are still growing in height from this movement. In some areas, where one plate is forced beneath the Earth's surface as it meets another plate, magma can sometimes find its way to the surface and create volcanoes.

Volcanoes and earthquakes have affected Italy throughout its history, from the famous eruption of Vesuvius and the destruction of Pompeii in AD 79, to the major Assisi earthquake in 1997. The most recent dramatic volcanic eruption was Mount Etna's outpouring in 2002.

CASE STUDY
SAN GIULIANO EARTHQUAKE

On 31 October 2002 there was an earthquake of 5.4 on the Richter scale in the village of San Giuliano in the Molise region. Most of the 29 deaths occurred within the Francesco Iovine School. The school had been built in the 1950s, before there were strict building regulations for areas that were likely to suffer earthquakes. During this period, poor design and shoddy materials were used. The concrete roof was too heavy, and within seconds the poorly constructed walls gave way and the roof crashed down, killing 26 pupils and their teacher. Other, much older buildings in the village suffered little or no damage.

The volcano on Stromboli island erupts several times an hour. It has been erupting this frequently for the last 160,000 years!

The ruins of Pompeii attract tourists who want to see the remains of this once-thriving Roman town.

VOLCANOES, PLATES AND MOUNTAINS

CASE STUDY
MOUNT ETNA

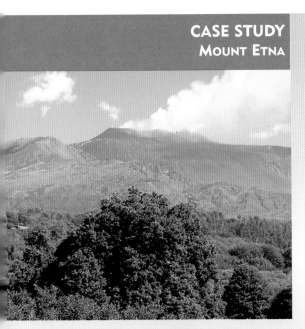

Ash and steam rise from Mount Etna – a constant threat to people living on its slopes.

Mount Etna, on the island of Sicily, is Europe's largest land-based volcano. It is located where the African and Eurasian plates meet. Etna erupts frequently. One million people live on the flanks of the volcano, attracted by the very fertile soils found there. They have learned to live with the constant threat of eruption from Etna. There was a major eruption period between 1992 and 1993 and in 2002 another period of volcanic activity occurred.

The volcano had shown signs of activity during the summer of 2002 and then on 27 October it erupted. This eruption was accompanied by many earthquakes, which continued for several days, reaching up to 4.3 on the Richter Scale. During the eruption, two streams of lava flowed down the north and south slopes of the volcano. Magma was propelled up to 300 metres into the air, and large areas of pine forest were set on fire by the hot lava. Heavy ash falls covered nearby villages and the town of Catania, and about 100 homes were damaged by earthquakes. In an effort to minimise the potential damage, 1,000 people were evacuated from their homes. Channels were dug to try and divert lava from villages, and water-carrying planes were placed on standby in order to put out fires.

RIVERS

Rivers that originate in the Alps, such as the Ticino and Po, have large basins and flow across the Po Plain to the sea. These rivers flow all year round, fed by rains in autumn and spring, and by melting glaciers in summer.

In the peninsula section of Italy rivers flow east and west from the Appennine watershed (boundary between drainage basins). As the peninsula is narrow these rivers are much shorter than those in the north. The flow of rivers such as the Ofanto in southern Italy depends entirely on rainfall, which can be heavy during spring and autumn, causing flash flooding. However, in the summer, rainfall can be so low that the rivers dry up completely.

PROBLEMS OF LOW FLOW

Italy's climate is characterised by summer drought, especially in the south. This problem has become worse over the last decade, partly due to global warming and partly because there has been a 25 per cent decline in annual average rainfall.

The water supply system, particularly in the south, is very inefficient. Approximately 60 per cent of Italians suffer some form of water shortage for

LEFT: A waterfall in the Alps flows into a plunge pool on its way down to the plains.

BELOW: Low flow in a river in Tuscany.

three months of the year. To combat this problem, aqueducts have been built to transfer water from the wetter areas in the mountains to the drier regions of the south such as Basilicata and Puglia, which receive only 550mm of rain each year. The Puglia Aqueduct transfers water from springs in the Appennines to Puglia via 247km of pipeline and through numerous tunnels.

FLOODING

With an increase in extreme weather conditions linked to global warming, Italy has suffered several disastrous floods over the last decade, including those in the Piemonte Region in 1994 when 94 people were killed. In 2000 the Ticino and Po rivers flooded in the north of Italy and 20 people were killed. At the same time 15 campers were killed in a flash flood in the south of the country. Part of the problem is that there has been an increase in building on the floodplain. This means that the land surface is cemented over and can no longer absorb water. There has also been large-scale deforestation on mountain slopes. This results in less rainfall being intercepted and absorbed by trees. Instead it speeds over the surface to the rivers and floods occur. Coupled with this the surface water picks up soil particles and transports them to the river where they add to the river bed, raising it and making the river more likely to flood.

This dried up river near Malazzo, Sicily, shows the impact of a summer drought.

2002 DROUGHT

In 2002 Italy suffered the worst drought for 50 years.

IMPACTS OF DROUGHT
- Farmers lost £2.8 billion, with thousands of hectares of crops destroyed.
- Hospitals ran out of water and had to get the fire brigade to transport some.
- Low lake levels, even in north of country.
- Water was being stolen and then resold.
- Areas of desertification increased in the south.
- People in towns often had water on tap for only a couple of hours a day.

SOLUTIONS
- Urgent repairs to existing water supply systems to reduce losses through leakage.
- Education campaign to encourage more sustainable use of water.
- Change in crop types to ones that require less water.
- Legislation to encourage industries to recycle water.
- Set up planned measures for rationing for future droughts.
- Replant watersheds to encourage retention of water within the landscape.
- Reintroduce terracing to help absorb rainfall naturally.

The Dora Baltea forms a tributary of the River Po, as it flows from the Alps.

The River Po is the longest river in Italy. It flows for 650km from its source in the western Alps to its delta on the Adriatic Sea in the east of the country. Its main tributaries also have their source in the Alps and include the Ticino, Adda and Dora Baltea rivers. The Po's drainage basin covers 70,000km² and forms 24 per cent of Italy's land surface. The area has a population of 16 million inhabitants and 44 per cent of it is used for farming. Over half of the crops are irrigated using water from the Po and its tributaries. Water is also extracted from the river for domestic and industrial use.

UPPER COURSE

The upper reaches of the Po have steep slopes, where the river flows at high speed and there is much erosion. In the first 35km of its channel, the River Po falls 1,700 metres with many rapids and waterfalls. This energy is harnessed by hydroelectric power (HEP) stations and within its basin there are 269 of them! The River Adda has eight HEP stations in its upper reaches. The dams linked to the power stations have caused changes to the river ecosystems as they have altered the water flow. Another problem is the fact that material eroded from the Alps by the fast-flowing river is dropped as the river loses energy on entering the reservoirs behind the dams. These reservoirs are gradually filling up with sediment and cannot store as much water.

MIDDLE SECTION

From Turin, the Po crosses its huge plain. It is here that human impact is greatest. The river used to meander across the floodplain but now for much of its course it has been straightened and held in by levees (embankments) to prevent the river from flooding and changing its course. This means that in times of high water flow the river cannot absorb the excess on its floodplain, which is now used for industry, housing and intensive agriculture. Irrigated rice farming is important here and the regular applications of chemical fertiliser have meant that there is a run-off of nitrates into the river, causing pollution. There are many chemical pollutants from the industries that line the river in Milan and Turin. Another source of pollution comes from domestic sewage. Until 2004, Milan still pumped most of the city's untreated human waste into the river from where it flows down to the delta.

THE DELTA

The Po Delta is where much of the material eroded from the Alps and Appennines is deposited. Farmland has been reclaimed from its marshes over the last 300 years and it is a productive rice-growing area. Fish farming of sea bass and shellfish is also an important industry (although this has been affected by pollution from the cities of the plain).

When the River Po reaches Turin, it flows past many industrial buildings. Pollution can be a major problem here.

However, the delta is also an important area for wildlife, particularly breeding and migrating birds. There has been conflict as there are moves to allow some of the reclaimed land to flood once again to provide an increasingly rare wetland habitat. This is not popular with farmers! Conservation tourism is seen as a way of providing new jobs within the proposed Po Delta National Park.

There is now a government-funded Po Basin Plan which is carrying out research and monitoring of the River Po. Eventually, this will lead to tougher pollution legislation and more sustainable ways of managing the river's channel.

Tourists wait for a boat to take them on to the Po Delta, where they will see rare wetland ecosystems.

CLIMATE

Italy has a wide range of climates, from the cool alpine region in the north to the warm Mediterranean peninsula region with its summer droughts. Regional winds can affect the climates of some areas. The Sirocco Wind is a hot, dry wind that blows from the deserts of North Africa in the summer and can add to the problems of Italy's summer drought. In spring, areas within the south and in Sardinia can be affected by the Mistral Wind, a cold, dry wind that blows off the continent of Europe and is sometimes responsible for extensive crop damage.

MOUNTAIN CLIMATES

In the Alps and in the Appennines the climate changes with altitude. Broad-leaved deciduous trees such as oaks grow in the valleys, where the climate is less harsh with warmer temperatures. Further up the mountains pine trees grow, which can cope with the colder and windier conditions found there. Above 2,000m (the treeline), it is too windy and cold for any trees to grow, but there are alpine meadows made up of grasses and flowering plants. Above these, but below the snowline, is a zone of alpine tundra with waterlogged soils in which mosses, lichens and tussock grasses grow.

In the summer, heat can build up above the south-facing slopes of the Alps and there are many thunderstorms, which give this area its peak rainfall.

CASE STUDY
SEVERE STORMS IN NORTHERN ITALY

On 4 August 2002, there was a particularly severe thunder and hail storm on the northern Po Plain. There had been a heat wave and the strong, upward movement of air caused violent thunderstorms with gales, heavy rain and hail. Hailstones weighing up to 700g were recorded – the same weight as four cricket balls! About 20 per cent of the fruit and olive harvest was destroyed, and vineyards near Lake Garda were severely damaged. Trees were blown down across roads and railways, and electricity supplies were disrupted. Hundreds of cars were damaged and 30 people were injured by hailstones.

The upper reaches of the Val D'Aosta are bare, while meadow plants thrive lower down.

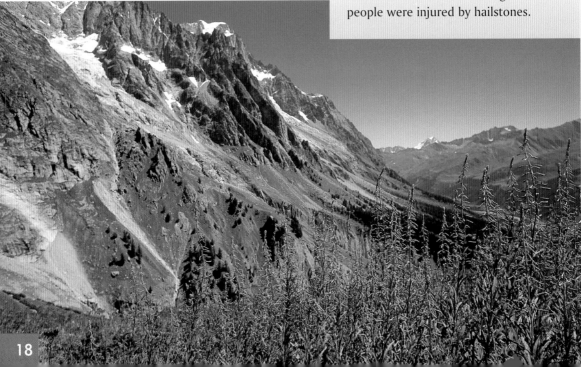

THE NORTHERN PLAIN

The large Northern Plain is surrounded on three sides by mountains and the Appennine Range prevents the warm sea breezes reaching the area. Autumn and winter are also characterised by fogs forming over the moist land. There are few strong winds here because the area is sheltered by the surrounding mountains, so the fog does not readily disperse. In the summer months there is a build up of heat, leading to strong, upward movements of air, causing many thunderstorms. The natural vegetation of this relatively flat plain includes moisture-loving willows and alders.

COASTAL AREAS

The coastal areas of Italy have a smaller temperature range than the interior regions. The Mediterranean Sea heats up slowly during the summer and releases this heat during the winter. It has the effect of keeping the temperatures of the coastal areas more even.

The eastern coasts are cooler than those of the west because the prevailing winds come from the north-east and tend to be

colder. The Mediterranean Sea on the eastern side of Italy (the Adriatic) is shallower and so does not store heat so well. The winds from over this part of the Mediterranean Sea do not even out the temperatures as well as those in the west.

TEMPERATURE AND RAINFALL

KEY:
Temperature
Rainfall

Long, hot summers and sandy beaches attract large numbers of holidaymakers to the Mediterranean coasts.

Marble has been extracted from quarries around Carrara for over 2,000 years.

Italy is quite a young country in term of its geology, and it is because of this that it does not have large deposits of minerals and ores. In the past, this lack slowed up Italy's development. The country has declining reserves of oil and gas and very little in the way of coal deposits. However, it does have thriving timber and fishing industries.

RAW MATERIALS

Volcanic activity has left large deposits of sulphur, such as at Barrafranca on the island of Sicily. Sulphur is used mainly in the manufacture of sulphuric acid. This is an important material in the paint industry and in the manufacture of explosives. Bauxite ore, from which aluminium is made, is mined on the Gargano Peninsula in eastern Italy. Apart from feldspar, which is used in the glass and ceramic industry, the mineral deposits are very small and Italian industry relies heavily on imports.

Over time heat and pressure deep underground have changed limestone deposits into marble. The finest white marble in the world is found at Carrara, in Tuscany, where it has been quarried since Roman times. It was used by Michelangelo for his statue of David and is still the marble of choice for many modern sculptors.

FORESTRY

Italy has 5 per cent of the world's cork oak forests. Around 2,400 tonnes of cork are produced each year, and Italy is the third most important producer after Portugal and Spain. Cork oaks are found especially in the Lombardia region. A cork oak does not produce cork until it is 20 years old and usually lives for 150 years. The cork comes from the outer bark, which is stripped away with great care and taken away to be processed. Over the next 5 years, the tree will grow a new outer layer, which can then be harvested again.

Around 33 per cent of Italy is forested, compared with about 11 per cent of the UK, and timber is an important resource for Italy. It is harvested mainly in the northern half of the country. The timber sector contributes 10 per cent to the national economy.

This timber yard in Piemonte processes trees that have been harvested in the region.

Some older forests are owned and run by the community, such as in the Val di Fiemme, in the south-eastern Alps. Harvesting the trees is carried out in small areas, which are clear-felled, prepared and then replanted. There is a move within these community forests towards multiple use of the forest area (see box on this page). This has already been happening in the publicly owned forests, but the aim in the community forests has been mainly timber production.

FISHING

Fishing is an important industry in Italy, especially around the islands of Sicily and Sardinia. Here sardines and blue fin tuna are caught and processed. However, there is growing concern about the level of the fish stocks in the Mediterranean Sea and catches have been declining. The EU is proposing drastic cuts to the amount fishermen are allowed to catch in order to maintain fish stocks in the future.

FEATURES OF A MULTI-PURPOSE FOREST

- Some areas are used for commercial timber production.

- Access is allowed to the public for recreation activities such as fishing, trekking and fungi harvesting.

- Some areas are designated as habitat reserves, where minimal management takes place. The aim of this is to support local wildlife.

- In a larger forest, there may also be a visitor centre.

Tuna and octopus for sale in a fish market, in Palermo, Sicily.

FISH CATCHES IN THE MEDITERRANEAN, 2005

Source: Eurostat, 2007

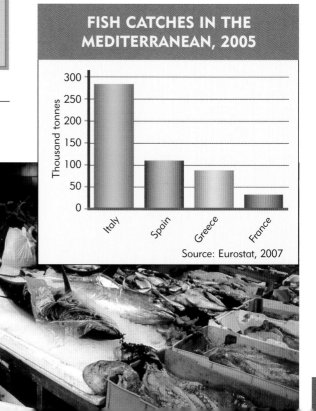

ENERGY

Italy has a high rate of energy consumption linked to its strong economy. However, the country has little in the way of fossil fuel reserves and is very dependent on imports for its energy supplies. Italy is trying to rely less heavily on imports of fossil fuels, partially because several of the countries upon which it depends are in the less politically stable areas of the world such as North Africa and the Middle East. Italy has also signed up to the Kyoto Agreement, which means that it is committed to reducing carbon emissions (linked to fossil fuel use) over the next decade.

COAL, OIL AND GAS

Italy has very little coal of its own and has to import it from South Africa, Indonesia and Australia. Coal makes up only 8.3 per cent of the energy demand and is used mainly in electricity generation. Italy is one of the largest oil consumers in Western Europe but 95 per cent of the oil consumed is imported, largely from North Africa and the Middle East. Natural gas is also imported from countries such as Russia and Norway by pipeline. There is also a pipeline from North Africa under the Mediterranean Sea to Sicily.

Italy does have some oil and gas reserves of its own. Oil is found on the island of Sicily and offshore. New onshore reserves are being developed at Val d'Agri, in the southern Appennines, and a pipeline has been built to connect it to the Taranto refinery. Gas fields are found mainly in the Po Valley, and others are located in the Adriatic Sea.

NUCLEAR POWER

Although Italy has four nuclear power plants, none of them are producing electricity. After the disaster at Chernobyl in the former USSR in 1986, Italians voted in 1987 to abandon nuclear power. The power stations have been maintained as they contain harmful wastes, which must be monitored. There have been recent moves by the Italian government to allow the power plants to once again be used to produce electricity, especially because they produce no carbon emissions and would help in keeping to the Kyoto Agreement.

RENEWABLE ENERGY

Hydroelectric Power (HEP) is the most important of Italy's renewable energy resources. Although expensive to build and having a considerable impact on the mountain ecosystems, once they are up and running HEP stations provide a sustainable form of power.

This oil refinery at Taranto processes mostly imported oil.

POWER FROM BENEATH THE EARTH'S SURFACE

Italy led the world in geothermal power production when the first geothermal power plant was commissioned in 1915 in Larderello and it remained the only one in the world until 1958! At Larderello, water is pumped at high pressure from deep, heated, underground sources and as it rises to the surface, pressure is released and steam is formed, which is used to drive turbines to create electricity.

Wind generators in Abruzzo provide a non-polluting alternative energy source to fossil fuels.

The Italian government is investing heavily in research into solar and wind power. The Vasto Plant in Abruzzo is the first large-scale solar power plant in Europe. The government has also recently launched its '10,000 Rooftops Programme', which aims to subsidise the construction of banks of photovoltaic (solar) cells on the roofs of domestic houses in order to reduce fossil fuel demand.

Wind power is being harnessed in the Appennine region and now there are plans to construct wind farms offshore in the south-west.

This HEP station in the Val d'Aosta in the Alps provides a clean, renewable energy supply for buildings in the surrounding area.

ENERGY SUPPLY, 2004 (% OF TOTAL)

Other renewables 5.6%
HEP 1.7%
Other 2.1%
Coal 8.3%
Natural gas 33.3%
Oil 49.0%

Source: International Energy Agency, 2007

ITALY'S ECONOMY

Beans and maize grow on a farm in Piemonte. Agricultural output is high in this area.

AGRICULTURE

Agricultural activities in Italy depend on the climate and landscape of the various regions, but other factors are also important, such as closeness to transport networks and markets, and the influence of European Union legislation. About 5 per cent of Italy's population work in the agricultural sector, but it only contributes 2 per cent of the nation's gross domestic product, or GDP.

MOUNTAINOUS FARMING

Farms tend to be smaller in upland areas and they are more likely to be family run. Steep slopes, a harsher climate and poor soils mean that mountainous areas are largely used for livestock rearing, rather than for

AGRICULTURAL LAND USE

- ▨ Irrigated area
- ◓ Major rice growing area
- ◔ Vines and olives
- ◔ Livestock rearing
- ◑ Cereal and dairy farming
- ● Citrus groves (oranges and lemons)

SWITZERLAND
AUSTRIA
FRANCE
SLOVENIA
Turin
CROATIA
San Remo
SAN MARINO
Ventimiglia
LIGURIAN SEA
N
CORSICA (FRANCE)
ADRIATIC SEA
Naples
SARDINIA
TYRRHENIAN SEA
MEDITERRANEAN SEA
SICILY

0   200km
0   100 miles

ECONOMIC STRUCTURE, 2005 (% GDP CONTRIBUTIONS)

Agriculture 2%
Industry 27%
Services 71%

Source: World Development Indicators, 2007

growing crops. In the Alpine region drought is not normally a problem, so lush grass can grow on the slopes. Cattle are reared here. In the drier Appennines sheep farming is more common, as sheep can thrive on poorer pasture. Vines are grown on south-facing slopes and fodder crops are grown for the animals in the Alps and Appennines.

THE IRRIGATED PLAINS

The most productive agricultural region is in the more industrial north, on the plain of the Po. The area receives rain all year and has fertile soils. Its productivity is enhanced by further irrigation, which leads to high yields of wheat and rice. Farms in this region are generally larger than those in the rest of Italy and there are more agribusinesses (large-scale commercial farms). Coastal plains near Naples also use irrigation and this, coupled with the fertile volcanic soils of the region, means that vegetables, fruit and cereals can be grown. Irrigation in north-eastern Sicily enables commercial production of lemons to take place.

CASE STUDY
FLOWER PRODUCTION AROUND SAN REMO

The area from Genoa to Ventimiglia on the Italian-French border is known as the *Riviera dei Fiori*, or the Coast of Flowers, with its centre at San Remo. The mild climate encourages the production of cut flowers such as carnations and roses, and pot plants, including geraniums. The hilly landscape has been adapted by cutting terraces to create small areas of flat land on which the flowers are grown. Most of the flower producers are very small firms who join together to form co-operatives to market their produce. San Remo's flower market is the most important in Southern Europe and has good links to the rest of the continent.

COASTAL AGRICULTURE

Around the coasts of Italy the traditional Mediterranean olive trees and vines are found. Further south, citrus groves also thrive, and in the north-west, flower production is important. Crops benefit from the very mild winters and warm, dry summers, although drought can be a problem.

CASE STUDY
WINE PRODUCTION

Italy has the third-largest area of vineyards in the world and produces about 20 per cent of the world's output of wine. The vines need brief but cold winters to kill off pests, and warm summers to ripen the grapes. They grow best on south- or south-east facing slopes and need to have well-drained soils. Much of Italy is used for growing vines. Red and white wines are produced, although most producers are small scale. There are more than 50,000 individual wine producers in Italy. Most family farms have a few vines on a small terrace of land just to provide wine for the family table. Italy's most famous wine is probably Chianti, a red wine produced in Tuscany but there are hundreds of others. Two popular wines, Soave and Valpolicella are also produced on an industrial scale and are widely exported.

Terraced vineyards in Barolo, Piemonte – an important region for wine production.

Leather jackets for sale on a market stall. Italy has many factories producing leather goods.

MANUFACTURING

Northern Italy is part of Europe's core area and is home to over half of Italy's manufacturing output. Its residents enjoy a higher income and lower unemployment rates than the South. The southern regions are known collectively as the *Mezzogiorno*, or 'land of the midday sun'. They are located on the peninsula of Italy and make up part of Europe's periphery; an outer region suffering from high unemployment. Although manufacturing and services are the largest sectors of the economy in this area, agriculture remains more important in terms of employment here than in the north.

THE NORTHERN POWERHOUSE

Northern Italy developed earlier than the south because of its trading links across the Alps and its fertile agricultural land in the Po Basin. Milan grew up because of this trade and is now the country's most important financial and business centre, home to the Italian Stock Exchange – the *Borsa*. Alpine streams provided early waterpower for the development of the textile industry. This eventually led to the development of the fashion industry based in Milan, which rivals Paris in its importance. Today Milan not only produces designer fashion but excels at manufacturing high-quality, mass-produced clothing. Famous Italian design houses include Valentino, Versace and Armani.

Wealth brought by the textile industry allowed the region to diversify its industries, and engineering design and manufacture became important in the twentieth century. Car manufacturing grew up around the city of Turin. Component manufacturers moved into the region to supply firms such as Fiat. Engineering continues to grow in this region because of a skilled workforce, good transport routes and the presence of similar companies.

CASE STUDY
FURNITURE CLUSTER AROUND TREVISO

Italy is famous for good quality, well-designed furniture. The industry is made up of many small firms, which specialise in different stages of product development. In Treviso, kitchen and office furniture is made with one company specialising in the production of the doors, another the work surfaces and yet another the handles. There are over 700 businesses in Treviso concerned with the manufacture of furniture!

GNI PER CAPITA (US$)

Source: World Development Indicators, 2007

This chemical factory in Bergamo has been built close to important fast road networks.

Although high-tech industries have suffered recently worldwide, they are an important sector within Italy's industries. In 2003 hi-tech manufacturing and service industries accounted for about 10.5 per cent of employment in Italy, similar to the EU average for the hi-tech sector at the time. These firms tend to cluster together in specialist groups, with financial IT firms located around Milan and those linked to the automobile industry around Turin.

Northern Italy has a wide range of industries and it is this diversity that will ensure that it continues to provide much of Italy's employment. Italy is known for excellent design and this, combined with a skilled workforce and good trade links, should ensure that the region continues to be a powerhouse for employment and production.

The Galleria, a huge shopping mall in Milan, sells all the famous designer labels.

CASE STUDY
UbiEst – Treviso

UbiEst is a high-tech firm located in Treviso. It specialises in gathering high-quality geographical map data, which it then organises into different formats for its customers. These maps can show whatever the customer wants, such as monuments or shops of a certain type. It is a small, specialist company and typical of firms found in the northern region.

THE *MEZZOGIORNO*

There continues to be a large gap in employment and income levels between the north and south of Italy. The south has lagged behind the north in development, having fewer resources. Deforestation occurred early in the region's history and allowed soil erosion to take place over hundreds of years. The soils of the region today are generally poor and thin. By the middle of the twentieth century, the *Mezzogiorno* region was falling ever further behind the north in terms of development. Transport links were poor and land ownership was in the hands of a few wealthy families.

In 1950, the Italian government created an organisation called the *Cassa per il Mezzogiorno*, in order to improve agriculture and transport links in the area, as well as trying to develop a modern industrial base. Over the 34 years of its existence the *Cassa* did improve agricultural methods and production by

AVERAGE UNEMPLOYMENT RATE BY REGION (%) 2005	
North-west	4.4
North-east	4.0
Central (including Rome)	6.4
South (including Sicily and Sardinia)	13.8
ITALY AS A WHOLE	7.7

Source: Eurostat

breaking up the large estates into individual farms. A new motorway was built, linking the south to the north, and state financed industry was set up in a triangle created by the three cities of Taranto, Brindisi and Bari. These industries were to attract others into the region. The quality of life did improve for southern Italians, but generally the gap between the regions did not get smaller.

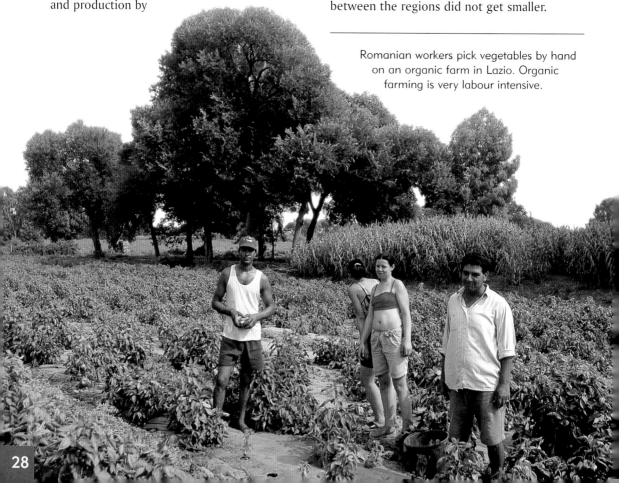

Romanian workers pick vegetables by hand on an organic farm in Lazio. Organic farming is very labour intensive.

Further government support since 1984 has still not put an end to the differences in income and employment levels. The north has attracted young people from the south and there has been continual migration from the rural areas of southern Italy to the factories of the north. Unemployment is still high in the region, with youth unemployment being particularly high. There is a national youth unemployment rate of 24 per cent, but in some of the southern regions it is over 50 per cent.

Since the 1990s there has been a change in the way help was given to the south. Large direct payments given in the past to the region do not seem to have resulted in much improvement. Now financial help, along with expert advice, is being targeted at specific projects and there must be some input from the local community or private investment.

In agricultural areas funding is available for farmers who wish to convert their holdings to organic farming, because the market for organic produce is growing. Italy has over a quarter of the European Union's organic farming, growing organic pasture, cereals and olives. Much of this funding has been in the less favoured areas of the south.

As the older heavy industries that were brought into the area by state funding become less profitable, it is important that other

Steelworks such as this one in Taranto were introduced by the government to help improve the economy of the south, but without success.

industries take their place. Developing the region's tourism potential is seen as an important method of generating revenue. Funding and training are available to help people set up, for example, small guest houses in areas such as Bari. The future for the south lies in diversifying its industries and giving its young people a reason to stay in the *Mezzogiorno*.

CASE STUDY
THE TARI PROJECT

Italy is a world leader in jewellery production and there is a well-established jewellery quarter in Naples. Although the old part of the city is the ideal location for jewellery shops, it is too cramped for manufacturing. Funding was given to develop a Jewellery Centre with exhibition space outside the city. The site had good road, rail and air links. Training workshops and a research facility have also been added. Jobs at the centre have increased 200 per cent since it was created.

TRADE AND TRANSNATIONAL COMPANIES

Italy is a member of the G8 – the group of leading industrial and economic powers in the world – and is very influential in global politics and the global economy. Italy's economy is the eighth-largest in the world, but its growth is slowing down.

One of the strengths of the Italian manufacturing industry is its attention to design and detail. This care for design is found in the many small, specialised firms that are typical of Italian industry. These firms are often family run, operating alongside similar enterprises in order to share expertise.

Globally there is a move towards Transnational Companies (TNCs). These are large companies with factories in more than one country that trade worldwide. Of the top 150 TNCs, 86 are based in the EU, but only 6 are located in Italy. People associate good design with Italian manufacturing industry and are willing to pay for that expertise. Smaller companies tend to be more innovative and TNCs often buy in their expertise.

Hundreds of containers packed with a huge variety of goods are lined up for export at the docks of Salerno, southern Italy.

CASE STUDY
BENETTON SUCCESS STORY

Benetton began in 1965 as a small, family-run clothing firm in Ponzano Veneto, northern Italy. The company sold good-quality, well-designed sweaters door-to-door. Later, the firm sold its product to independently owned shops under the Benetton name. Today, there are 5,000 stores in 120 countries worldwide. Benetton owns the 50 most important flagship stores in major cities such as Paris, New York, Osaka and Lisbon. About 3,500 people are directly employed by Benetton, and over 50,000 are employed by its sub-contractors. Up to 80 per cent of its clothing production still takes place in Italy, produced by sub-contractors such as Bronte Jeans, in Sicily. There have been some problems with sub-contractors in countries such as Turkey, where it is alleged that child labour has been employed. The company's magazine *Colors* reinforces its commitment to issues of global concern such as world hunger, and is published in six languages in 80 countries. Recently, the company has diversified away from its core clothing business into running motorway service stations and toll roads.

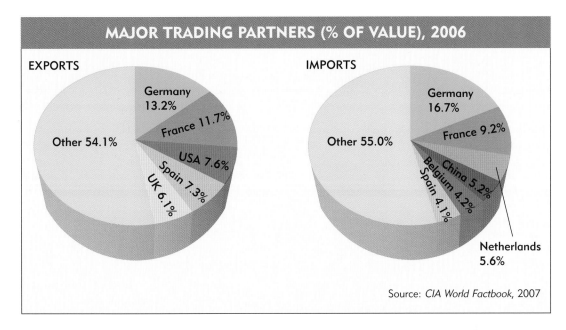

MAJOR TRADING PARTNERS (% OF VALUE), 2006

EXPORTS

Germany 13.2%
France 11.7%
Other 54.1%
USA 7.6%
Spain 7.3%
UK 6.1%

IMPORTS

Germany 16.7%
France 9.2%
Other 55.0%
China 5.2%
Belgium 4.2%
Spain 4.1%
Netherlands 5.6%

Source: *CIA World Factbook*, 2007

CASE STUDY
FIAT

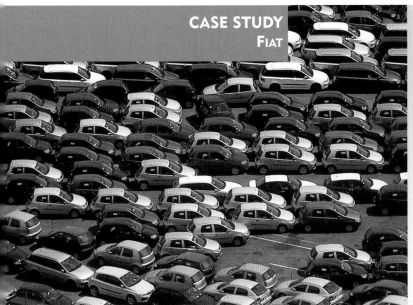

Fiat cars ready for export. Fiat is fighting to maintain its share of the European market.

Fiat, Italy's largest employer, was founded in Turin, in 1899. Initially the company employed 150 workers. Today Fiat employs 174,000 worldwide in over 100 countries. Although best known for car manufacturing, Fiat has diversified into producing lorries and tractors, publishing, insurance, metallurgy, aviation, robotics and manufacturing lubricants.

Its car division now includes Fiat, Alfa Romeo, Lancia, Ferrari and Maserati. These cars are either produced by Fiat itself or under license in countries such as Italy, Brazil, Argentina, Morocco, China and India.

Recently the company has suffered from foreign competition and its market share within Europe has fallen from 14 per cent in 1991 to less than 7 per cent in 2003. In October 2002, 7,600 Italian car workers were laid off and most of the Fiat factories were only working for 75 per cent of the time. Some of Fiat's factories are in the south of the country and if these close there is very little other employment. The company has debts as a result of buying other companies in order to diversify and must now make a decision whether to carry on as a car manufacturer within a larger organisation such as General Motors of the USA or to sell off the car division and concentrate on its other interests.

EU and Italian flags fly together outside the Senate in Rome.

Today Italy is a republic, but the country has had few periods of political stability. Since 1945 Italy has had 60 changes of government – there have been 10 changes since 1993! Italy has one of the world's largest economies. The country contributes to and participates in a broad range of international organisations.

THE UNITED NATIONS

Italy joined the United Nations (UN) in 1955 and is the sixth-largest contributor. It participates in peace-keeping in the trouble spots of the world, giving economic and humanitarian aid to less economically developed countries (LEDCs), and also helping with the promotion of development. Italy is also the top contributor to the programme against organised crime and promoted the formation of the International Criminal Court of Justice, which is part of a worldwide fight against international crime groups such as the Mafia (see page 47). In 2007 Italian troops were active in UN peace-keeping missions in Lebanon and other areas of the Middle East.

THE EUROPEAN UNION

Italy was a founder member of the European Union (EU), whose aims include the promotion of economic and social progress, European citizenship, ensuring freedom and security, and the promotion of Europe throughout the world.

Although Italy is a major contributor to the EU, the country also derives many benefits from its membership. Italy has benefited from EU funding for its problem areas, mainly in the *Mezzogiorno* region and the southern islands. The development of organic farming in Sicily (see page 29) largely came about because of EU funding, supporting farmers whilst they set up their organic farms and helping to improve irrigation. Many other areas get funding under the Less Favoured Areas (LFA) schemes. In mountainous regions where farms are small and uneconomic, for example, grants are given to encourage young farmers to stay on the land and maintain it. To have access to the grants they must follow environmentally friendly farming methods such as crop rotation and tree planting. Cities also benefit from funding by the EU. Palermo, in Sicily, has received money to help develop a sustainable public transport system.

The naval base at Spezia is an important base for NATO ships.

ITALY'S MEMBERSHIP OF ORGANISATIONS

Italy belongs to the following international organisations:

EU   European Union. An economic union of European countries. In 2007 there were 27 member countries.

UN   United Nations. This group works to maintain peace and encourage development. 191 countries belong to the UN.

G8   The Group of 8 more economically developed countries promoting international trade and relations with less economically developed countries.

WEU   Western European Union. This is an economic grouping of 10 members. It was set up originally to form a defensive league but now aims to integrate other more easterly countries of Europe into a larger alliance.

WTO   World Trade Organisation. This organisation governs rules of trade between nations. There are 151 members.

NATO North Atlantic Treaty Organisation. This is a group of 26 members who work together to provide collective defence and security.

OECD Organisation for Economic Co-operation and Development. A group of 30 members committed to the market economy and democratic government.

OSCE Organisation for Security and Co-operation in Europe. This group is made up of 56 nations involved in security related issues such as arms control.

TRANSPORT

Italy depends on good transport links to allow goods and people to reach their destinations. Northern Italy has a complex system of rail and road networks, but transport systems are not as well developed in the south. In the past the difference was even more pronounced until large amounts of government aid were made available from the late 1950s onwards to help build up the region's transport routes.

ON THE ROADS

Italy has 6,621km of motorway, leading from the Alpine tunnels and passes in the north to a hub around Milan. From here they radiate out to the coasts and there are two main motorway links to the south. The most important is the *Autostrada del Sol* (Highway to the Sun), which runs all the way down to the toe of Italy.

Italians have one of the highest levels of car ownership in the world, with more than 33.7 million on the road. Italians are known for their individuality and love of speed, but unfortunately this results in a road death toll nearly twice that of the UK – a country with a similar-sized land mass and population. Small cars dominate the Italian market because they are much easier to park than larger cars in Italy's congested city centres.

These girls will be able to beat the traffic on their Italian-built scooter.

A new stretch of *autostrada* (motorway), in Sicily. Such transport links may help improve the economy of southern Italy.

CASE STUDY
FERRARA – A CITY FOR CYCLISTS

The city of Ferrara is located on the flat Po Plain, which is ideal for cyclists. It is part of the Cities for Cyclists Network and does everything to encourage the use of bicycles. Although car ownership is high, many people in Ferrara drive to work and then use a bicycle for shopping or going out for lunch. About 90 per cent of the population uses a bicycle at some time. The city has created many cycle tracks to access as much of the city as possible, including a track that goes round the city walls. In some hotels in Ferrara, the price per room includes the use of a bike!

This high-speed train in the central station of Rome is about to depart for Milan.

RAILWAYS

Italy has 19,460km of railways. There are high-speed links between Rome, Florence and Milan. Several cities have metro lines (underground railways), including Genoa, Milan and Rome.

TRANSPORT BY AIR AND SEA

The national airline is Alitalia, which had a fleet of 179 aircraft in 2005, operating 2,784 weekly flights to 110 airports worldwide. In that year Alitalia carried 24 million passengers. Italy has 25 main commercial airports. The busiest is in Rome, with 27.2 million passengers passing through each year.

Italy has a large merchant fleet and has many ports, the most important being those of Genoa on the Mediterranean Sea, Trieste on the Adriatic Sea and Augusta in Sicily.

TRANSPORT NETWORKS

Key:
- —— Main roads
- ······· Railways
- ✈ International airports
- ⛴ Ports

FRANCE

LIECHTENSTEIN
SWITZERLAND

SLOVENIA
Trieste

Turin · Milan · Verona · Venice
Ferrara
Genoa · Bologna
SAN
MARINO
Pisa · Florence

CROATIA

LIGURIAN
SEA

ADRIATIC SEA

N

CORSICA
(FRANCE)

Rome

Bari
Naples
Brindisi
Taranto

SARDINIA

TYRRHENIAN
SEA

Cagliari

MEDITERRANEAN SEA

Palermo · Messina
SICILY · Catania

0 ———— 200km
0 ———— 100 miles

CASE STUDY
INTEGRATED TRANSPORT IN GENOA

The port city of Genoa developed a new Urban Transport Plan in 2000 with the aims of encouraging more use of public transport, and of developing better links between bus, car and rail systems. In 2002 it was estimated that nearly 50 per cent of daily traffic movements within the city were made by local public transport.

Features of Genoa's integrated transport system include:

- Buses have satellite systems that enable them to transmit their position and relay it to screens at bus stops to keep passengers informed

- Priority lanes are provided for buses

- Rail and bus timetables are linked

- An electric bus connects the Park and Ride areas to the city centre

- There are toll charges for cars to enter the city centre.

URBAN ITALY

Italy has a long history of urbanisation, with cities such as Rome and Florence existing from before the Roman Empire. During the Middle Ages many of the cities became independent city states under the influence of powerful families such as the Medici of Florence. Their wealth grew mainly by trade and Italy became one of the most cultured regions in Europe. From the sixteenth century Italy's powerful cities declined in power as other countries such as Spain and Austria took control over the country.

After the unification of Italy in 1861, Rome became the capital. Since that time there has been much rural-urban migration to cities, especially from the impoverished farmlands of the south. Today these cities have to cope with the problems of modern urban living, often with historic city centres that require conserving and protecting. Italy does not want to stay in the past and there have been many urban initiatives to improve the quality of life for city residents, whilst preserving a city's historical heritage.

ROME

Known as the 'Eternal City' Rome has an urban history of over 2,000 years. It was built near a major crossing point of the River Tiber on seven low hills overlooking the floodplain. Today the city is a mixture of expanding modern suburbs with ancient buildings at its core. Rome has 82 per cent of its working population in the service industries such as local government and tourism. Rome's manufacturing industry tends to focus on small specialist firms in fashion accessories and, more recently, high-tech industry including software design and aerospace.

The city has many problems arising from its growth. One of the most obvious is traffic congestion. Most of its service industry is based in the city centre. As most of the population lives in the suburbs, this means huge daily flows of people and cars. At its historic centre the city has many narrow streets, which are not suited to today's motor traffic. With a lack of off-road car parking

TELECOMMUNICATIONS DATA

(Per 1,000 people)	
Mainline phones	427
Mobile phones	1,232
Internet users	478

Source: World Bank

ABOVE: A busy street junction in Rome. All of Italy's major cities have traffic congestion.
LEFT: Rome's cityscape provides a view of ancient, historical monuments, standing alongside modern buildings.

areas, the congestion is made worse by people parking cars on the streets and making them even narrower.

To reduce traffic public transport needs to be improved. The metro system only covers limited parts of the city and is not coping with increasing numbers of passengers. However planned improvements are underway. Most buses, with the exception of the electric ones in Rome's centre, are highly polluting but are well used. In 2000, Rome's ageing tram system was given a boost when 28 new trams were ordered with the aim of getting more people out of their cars and using public transport to get to work. Experiments have been carried out with teleworking, so that some local government employees can work from home, reducing car traffic in the centre.

Many of Rome's high-rise blocks are cramped and shoddily-built, leading to a poor quality of life for those who live there.

SOCIAL PROBLEMS

A housing shortage in the 1960s and 1970s resulted in poor-quality high-rise flats being built in Rome, and it is here that there are now social problems. These areas have high unemployment levels. Many of the inhabitants are immigrants, so there is also racial tension. Large amounts of graffiti are found all over these estates but now it is found even on the ancient monuments of the historic centre. The city government has set up an Office of City Decorum to try and clean up buildings and to change youth behaviour.

MILAN

Milan is the economic capital of Italy and has a wide range of industries both in manufacturing (such as engineering and textiles) and in services especially finance, design, publishing, and research and development. It is the hub of the road and rail network in northern Italy and is an important commercial centre, home to the world's first shopping mall – the *Gallaria Vittoria Emanuele* begun in 1865!

With industrial suburbs and heavy traffic, the city suffers from severe air pollution. Several times in 2002 the pollution levels were five times the permitted maximum. Cars were banned from the city on Sundays and people were encouraged to use the trams in an effort to reduce the pollution.

Many people are moving away from the city to live in more rural areas and the remaining population is ageing. About 6 per cent of the city is over 75, and in the decaying northern part of the city 27 per cent are over 65. In order to support this increasingly dependent population the city has begun a project to convert derelict buildings into service centres for the elderly. These include a day centre and a unit to help the elderly remain independent.

GENOA

Genoa is an important port in the north of Italy. Towards the end of the twentieth century, port activity declined as Italy's industries became more service based. Port-based industries closed and the city's unemployment figures rose. Genoa is a culturally mixed city, and there were increasing racial tensions and a rising crime rate in the deprived areas next to the port.

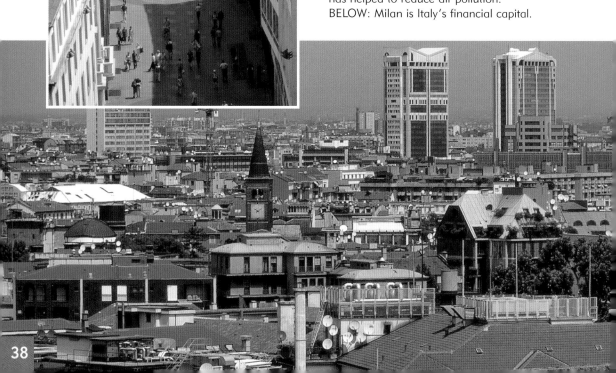

LEFT: Pedestrianisation in parts of central Milan has helped to reduce air pollution.
BELOW: Milan is Italy's financial capital.

Genoa's new harbourfront is dominated by a unique mast sculpture by artist Renzo Piano.

In 1992 the Old Port area was renovated. A world-class aquarium was built and the port buildings converted into bars and restaurants to attract tourists.

Money from the EU was later used to bring new life to the run-down historic centre with the development of the Urban Observatory (a research and information centre) in a restored convent and an urban studies facility in a redundant church. These projects have improved the area and encouraged other developments.

In 2004 Genoa became Europe's City of Culture with the aim of further regenerating its harbour area and linking it to the restored historic centre.

NAPLES

Naples was once an important port in the south of Italy. Although one of the poorest cities in the EU it is still the most important city in the *Mezzogiorno* region. Its heavy industries, set up by the Italian government, have mainly closed leaving the area with high unemployment, often over 50 per cent.

Corruption and the siphoning of money by the Mafia (a criminal organisation – see page 47) has meant that many redevelopment projects did not get started, and many of those that did were not completed. A new mayor started a new phase of redevelopment in the mid-1990s. Most work has been done in the port and central areas because it is hoped that it will stimulate tourism and therefore create more jobs. An increased police presence on the streets led to a huge drop in crime and tourism grew by 40 per cent as visitors began to feel safe in the city. Many museums and palaces have now been restored and opened to the public. The main square has been paved and pedestrianised to act as a vibrant core to the area.

URBAN POPULATION

% of total population

Source: UN World Urbanisation Prospects, 2005
* = estimate

A dramatic sky over the Bay of Naples.

THE PEOPLE OF ITALY

Italy's population structure is changing. In about 30 years' time, most people will be over 60 years old.

Italy has a population of just over 58 million, but the country is now at a stage where its death rate is higher than its birth rate. This means that without immigration Italy's population will decline.

Life expectancy is increasing, with women expected to live to 83 years and men to 78. In 1960 there were about 5 million people over 65, in 2005 this had increased to over 11.7 million, forming 20 per cent of the total population. In contrast children aged 0–14 years now form only 14 per cent of the population. In the future this will mean that there will be fewer people of working age to support an increasing number of the elderly.

INTERNATIONAL EMIGRATION

During the nineteenth and twentieth centuries many Italians emigrated to find a better life in other European countries, the USA, South

MIGRATION WITHIN ITALY

For much of the twentieth century Italians in the south were attracted to the more affluent northern region, a movement that continues today although in far smaller numbers.

PUSH FROM THE SOUTH	PULL TO THE NORTH
High unemployment levels	Range of manufacturing/ service jobs
Very small uneconomic farms	Perceived better lifestyle
Poor soil and soil erosion	Jobs with regular wage rather than seasonal agricultural jobs
Lack of job opportunities other than farming	Higher wages

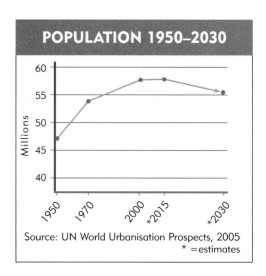

POPULATION 1950–2030

Source: UN World Urbanisation Prospects, 2005
* =estimates

America, Canada and Australia. Parts of many foreign cities such as Boston, USA, have 'Little Italy' districts. In some cases almost all the young people from a village would emigrate after hearing about how others were making a new life for themselves. It is thought that over 26 million Italians emigrated, largely from the depressed southern region but since the 1970s, as Italy has grown wealthier, this movement has largely stopped.

INTERNATIONAL IMMIGRATION

Italy's peninsula has a very long coastline, which makes it vulnerable to illegal immigration, especially from Albania and the countries of North Africa. In 2003, 3.85 per cent of Italy's population was foreign, mainly from Morocco and Albania. During that year, it received about 440,000 international immigrants. Most of the immigrants are unskilled and find work in the agricultural, construction and tourism industries. Often these are jobs that Italians do not want to do, but recently Italy has drafted some much stricter immigration laws to try to stem the flow of illegal immigrants. In future it is likely that there will be laws limiting employment prospects for immigrants in order to try and deter the purely economic migrants (people who migrate simply to obtain a better lifestyle).

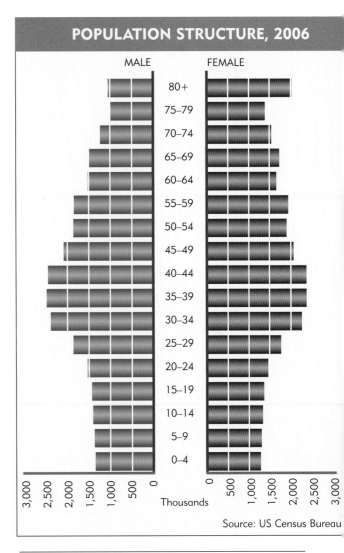

POPULATION STRUCTURE, 2006

MALE | FEMALE

80+, 75–79, 70–74, 65–69, 60–64, 55–59, 50–54, 45–49, 40–44, 35–39, 30–34, 25–29, 20–24, 15–19, 10–14, 5–9, 0–4

3,000 2,500 2,000 1,500 1,000 500 0 | 0 500 1,000 1,500 2,000 2,500 3,000

Thousands

Source: US Census Bureau

African migrants selling crafts on the streets.

ASYLUM SEEKERS

Italy has always offered asylum to people with a genuine fear of persecution in their home countries. In 1999 Italy received 18,450 asylum applications but by 2005 this had fallen to about 9,500 applicants, at least 36 per cent of whom were given some form of protection.

Girl scouts in Abruzzo. In Italy many scout groups include boys and girls.

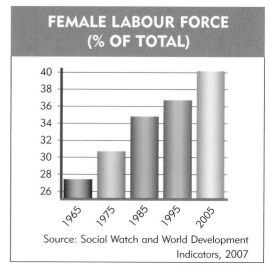

FEMALE LABOUR FORCE (% OF TOTAL)

Source: Social Watch and World Development Indicators, 2007

MARRIAGE AND FAMILY LIFE

On average, Italians get married at the age of about 28, and 75 per cent of people still get married in church. Italy's divorce rate is one of the lowest in Europe at 17 per cent (compared to 52 per cent in the UK). Women are now much more likely to work outside the home, and many decide not to have children or to delay when they have them. Italians love children, but today many couples are having fewer, with each woman on average producing 1.3 babies. This means that the birth rate has fallen to below population replacement level.

Family is very important to Italians and much of their social life revolves around the extended family, including grandparents and cousins. Once a baby is born, both parents can have three months at home on full pay.

Childcare is both expensive and difficult to find, so grandparents often step in to look after children whilst the parents are at work. Although church attendance is falling in Italy, 95 per cent of babies are still baptised into the Roman Catholic Church.

EDUCATION

At the age of six, all children begin at primary school, and they begin to learn a foreign language, usually English, by the age of seven. Secondary school is divided into two stages – the first is from the age of 11 to 14. Then children have a choice of schools from 14 to 18.

Rome's La Sapienza University is the largest in Italy.

In Italy people are living for longer and having fewer children. In the future there will be more old people than young ones.

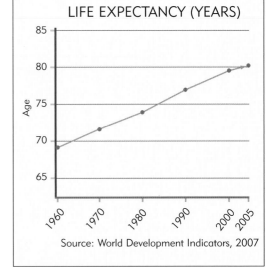

UNDER-FIVE MORTALITY RATE

Source: World Development Indicators, 2007

LIFE EXPECTANCY (YEARS)

Source: World Development Indicators, 2007

Many choose technical schools, which concentrate on administration, commerce and industrial practice. Other options include vocational schools, where students study crafts, and the more academic options of the classics, language or science schools. On completing their studies at 18 students leave with a diploma, which means they can go on to university.

There is high youth unemployment across much of Italy, so qualifications are seen as a necessity for getting any sort of job. Most young Italians live at home, largely because of cost, although some sons find that their mothers do not want to let them go. Young Italians therefore do not have a lot of privacy and they often regard cars as something they must have in order to have a bit of private space and the means of escape!

At 18 many young people progress to university, often in the nearest town so that they can live at home. Italy has 47 universities. Rome's La Sapienza is the largest, with 138,000 students. The lecture theatres are usually very crowded and students are lucky to get a seat.

HEALTHCARE

Italy has a good level of healthcare but this will be strained as the population ages. Italians live longer than almost any other nationality in Europe and they can expect to draw a pension at 56 or after working for 35 years. This is set to change – more people are living longer and in order for everyone to have a pension it must be taken at a later age. At the end of their lives, the elderly are usually looked after by their families. It is seen as a failure of the family if a parent has to move into a retirement home, but this may become more common as children move away in search of jobs.

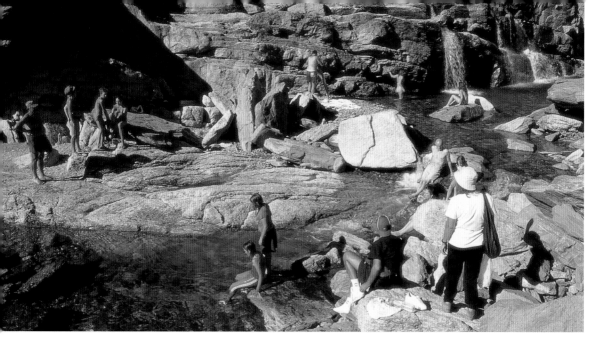

ITALIANS AND LEISURE

Italian leisure time mainly revolves around home and family, and 60 per cent of Italians spend two hours a day meeting friends and relatives. It is traditional in Italy, especially in the summer, for the family to go out together after the evening meal to walk up and down the local streets. Here they meet and talk to friends and local people to see what is going on in the area and to gossip. This evening parading is known as 'La Passeggiata' (which means 'The Walk'). The squares in towns are often buzzing late into the evening. Families may stop at a café for drinks of beer and coffee as part of La Passeggiata. The children may have a granita, a drink made from fresh fruit juice and crushed ice.

Visitors to Gran Paradiso National Park cool off by a lake.

Television viewing is very popular and 99 per cent of homes own at least one TV. Most of the population watches at least two hours of TV a day. RAI is the state-owned television company and has three stations, which offer the best quality programmes.

There is no truly national newspaper, but La Repubblica of Rome and the Corriere della Sera of Milan do cover some national issues. Over half of the population reads a newspaper at least once a week.

Film viewing remains popular, despite the ownership of video recorders and DVD players. Most large towns have several

La Passeggiata: people enjoy the nightlife at a restaurant in Lucca.

TELEVISION SETS PER 1,000 PEOPLE

Source: International Telecommunications Union

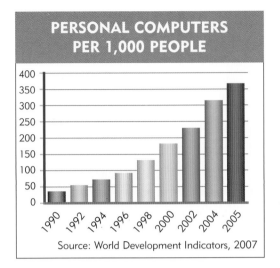

PERSONAL COMPUTERS PER 1,000 PEOPLE

Source: World Development Indicators, 2007

SPORT

Italians are passionate about football and it is the national sport. There are three leagues, with Serie A being the top division. Top teams include AC Milan, Inter Milan and Juventus.

There is now a growing interest in rugby, and in 2000 Italy joined Ireland, Wales, Scotland, England and France to form the Six Nations Championship.

Motor racing is another popular spectator sport. Italy has two Grand Prix racing circuits – the Imola Circuit in San Marino and the Monza Circuit near Milan.

Hunting is also popular and there are over 800,000 regular hunters in Italy. They shoot rabbits, wild boar and, more controversially, songbirds, which are often protected in other countries.

cinemas or a multi-screen. The Venice Film Festival, founded in 1932, is the oldest in the world.

Italians enjoy all kinds of music but are perhaps most associated with opera. The world-famous tenor, Luciano Pavarotti, did much to give Italian opera a high profile. There are many opera venues in Italy, including ones held in the open air such as at Verona. La Scala, in Milan, is the most famous opera house in Italy.

HOLIDAYS

In 2005, 24.2 million Italians took holidays involving a stay of 4 nights or more away from home. Of these, the majority were domestic holidays taken within Italy. When travelling abroad, France is the most popular destination followed by Spain. Many Italians enjoy camping and caravanning, and there are over 2,000 campsites in Italy, ranging from very basic ones to others that offer swimming pools, saunas and restaurants.

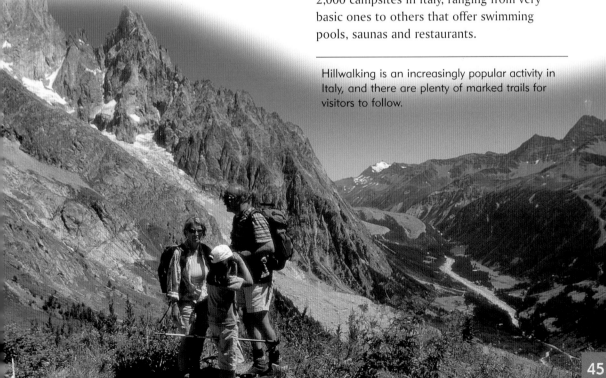

Hillwalking is an increasingly popular activity in Italy, and there are plenty of marked trails for visitors to follow.

ISLAND LIFE

Italy is largely a peninsula of southern Europe but it also has many islands within its territory, the largest of which are Sicily and Sardinia.

AEOLIAN ISLANDS

North of Sicily are the Aeolian islands, a group of volcanoes. One of them is Vulcano, which gave its name to all other volcanoes, but today it just rumbles and smokes. Visitors often go there for the famous hot mud baths. Lipari is the largest of the Aeolian islands and is the centre for ferries to and from the other islands in the group. One of its main products is pumice stone, for use in the home and as an industrial abrasive. Stromboli is the most isolated of the islands and is home to the world's most continuously active volcano. It still erupts about every 20 minutes and is a spectacular sight at night. The island's isolation meant that until the ferry and hydrofoil connections were made, many people left the island and emigrated to Australia in search of work and a better life. Stromboli has a population of 500 but because of its isolation, lack of space for development and its quite rainy climate, it does not attract mass tourism. Most people who visit this island do so to walk up the flanks of the volcano and look down into its fiery heart.

SICILY

Sicily is one of the most densely populated areas of Italy, having a total population of 5 million. The island has been ruled by Greeks, Romans, Arabs, Norman French and Spanish. The Sicilian accent still has an Arab influence and the people can trace their ancestors to a wide variety of nationalities. For many inhabitants of the island, they are Sicilian first and Italian second. Sicily is closer

Stromboli's traditional fishing industry continues alongside the island's increasingly important tourist industry.

geographically to Africa than to Milan, and it is in a good position within the Mediterranean Basin to have easy links with North African countries. There is only limited industry and the island suffers from very poor road and rail networks.

Industries already established there include textile industries and food processing. Sicily grows and exports citrus fruit especially lemons as well as a range of other agricultural produce. It relies heavily on irrigation but there are problems with the water supply due to government money meant for improvement going into the pockets of the Mafia (see box).

There were plans to build a bridge across the Straits of Messina to join Sicily with the mainland in order to speed up traffic links. It would have been 5km long and would have cost €4.6 billion. Sicilians said it might be better to first improve the roads, railways and water supplies on the island before carrying out these plans. The project was scrapped in 2006, mainly because of its high cost.

THE MAFIA

Sicily has very high unemployment levels and much of the money that has been provided by the EU or the Italian government has not found its way to the planned projects, partly because of the Mafia – a criminal organisation. The Mafia is involved in drug trafficking, prostitution, demanding money for protection for businesses and diverting government money into their own funds. Recently much has been done to try to reduce its influence by arresting and taking its leaders to court. People are now more confident and are speaking out against the organisation. It is hoped that international companies will then want to locate on the island.

A fruit stall in Palermo. Sicily's warm climate means that a wide range of fruit can be grown.

TOURISM

Italy has had a long history of tourism, dating back to the days of the Roman Empire when officials running the Empire would go to Rome for a business trip or to the country to rest and recuperate. In the eighteenth and nineteenth centuries Italy was one of the countries in the Grand Tour, a tour of Europe undertaken by aristocratic young people as part of their education. Today, Italy is an important destination for tourists, both within and beyond Europe.

Italy has a varied landscape, ranging from the snowy peaks of the Alps to the rocky coastline of Liguria. Tourists flock to visit the arid landscapes of the south, the sandy beaches on the Adriatic Sea and Italy's volcanoes, including Mount Etna. Popular tourist destinations include the great cities such as Venice for its canals, Florence for its art and architecture, and Rome for the Vatican City and the Coliseum. Archaeology is a tourist magnet with historic sites such as Pompeii (destroyed by the eruption of Vesuvius in AD 79) having 2.3 million visitors a year.

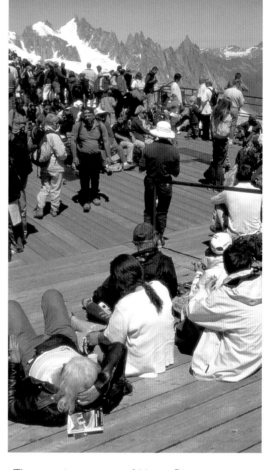

The stunning scenery of Monte Bianco attracts visitors during the winter and summer months.

For visitors to Lazio, the beautiful beaches are the top attractions.

TOURIST ARRIVALS, 2005	
France	76.0 million
Spain	55.6 million
USA	49.4 million
China	46.8 million
Italy	36.5 million

Souce: World Tourism Organisation, 2006

Tourism is the main source of income for cities such as Venice, although the city is sometimes in danger of being swamped by the huge numbers of visitors. In the height of summer the streets are so crowded that there is little of the magical experience that earlier travellers spoke of. The present Italian government realises that tourism is one of Italy's most important industries and is funding many projects to try to improve tourism income. This is especially true in the *Mezzogiorno*, where tourism is seen as an alternative to the dying heavy industry around the Bari, Brindisi, Taranto industrial area.

CASE STUDY
FLORENCE

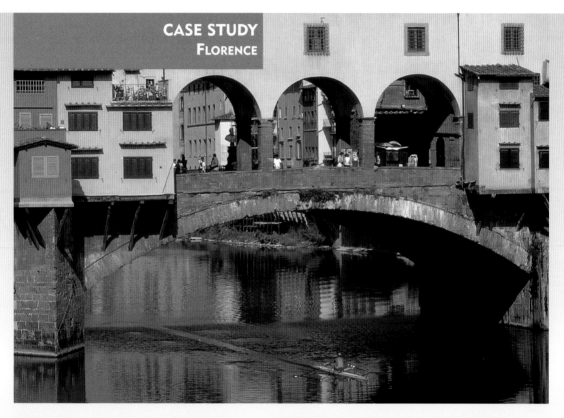

The Ponte Vecchio is one of Florence's most visited sites.

Florence is a city of the Renaissance period of the fifteenth century. Most of the buildings from this period are still in existence, and this is what makes Florence so attractive to visitors. The historic centre with its beautiful buildings filled with artwork such as Michelangelo's David now attracts 7 million tourists a year.

The huge numbers of tourists has created many problems for the city. Crowds gather around statues in museums and in the street, touching and climbing on them. The acid in human sweat eats away at the marble and chewing gum is trodden into the marble floors. The whole of the centre of Florence is of historical interest, and in 1982 it was designated a World Heritage Site. However, this was not enough to protect the city, and in the early 1990s the city council decided to draw up a Code of Conduct, which is given out to all tourists in the city to help them protect and appreciate its beauty. Tourist Police are employed to keep an eye on unruly behaviour. In the 1980s, the Uffizi, Italy's most important art gallery had up to 11,000 visitors a day! Today, daily numbers of visitors are restricted to 5,000. In the future the Council is considering charging entry fees to the historic city to pay for its maintenance and restoration.

THE ENVIRONMENT

Gran Paradiso was one of Italy's first national parks, protecting high Alpine mountains and valleys.

During the twentieth century, Italy became aware that its landscapes and wildlife were under threat from clearance for agriculture and urbanisation. In 1922, Italy's first national park was established in the Appennines, the Abruzzo National Park. Today, 10 per cent of Italy is under state protection and 5 per cent of the land has national park status. Italy's regional and national parks attract more than 17 million visitors a year and some are now having problems with visitor traffic in the summer.

MAIN NATIONAL PARKS

LIECHTENSTEIN AUSTRIA
SWITZERLAND Stelvio N
SLOVENIA
Dolomiti
Bellunesi
Gran
Paradiso CROATIA
SAN BOSNIA -
MARINO HERZEGOVINA
Foreste
Casentinesi
CORSICA Maiella
(FRANCE) Abruzzo Gargano

SARDINIA

Capo
Aspromonte Rizzuto

● National parks SICILY
0 200km
● Marine reserve 0 100 miles

Italy is now protecting many of its wild coastal areas, such as in the marine reserve of Circeo National Park, Lazio.

Horseriding is just one of many activities that can be undertaken in Abruzzo National Park.

Situated just two hours' drive away from Rome, Abruzzo National Park is one of the most visited in Italy. It is the oldest and the largest of the parks, covering 50,000 hectares of mountain peaks, rivers, lakes and forest. It contains 45 per cent of Italy's species of mammals and over 2,000 different plant species. The animals include the 'big seven' – bear, wolf, chamois, red deer, roe deer, eagle and lynx – which receive full protection within the park.

The park authorities realised that a balance was needed between protecting the animals and allowing public access, and so now the park is divided into four zones. The first is a core zone, where there is no human activity and the wildlife is left totally alone. The second zone is the General Reserve, which can be accessed with a permit. The third is the Protection Zone, where people can visit and enjoy the landscape and walking trails. This acts as a buffer to the fourth zone, the Development Zone, where hotels and restaurants can be located, and where some limited extraction of resources such as trees is allowed. Even here all development is small scale and there are no large hotels or any ski lifts.

National parks tend to cover large areas and aim to protect, and conserve landscapes and the wildlife within. They also promote access for recreation, which can conflict with conservationist aims. A certain amount of economic activity takes place within the parks, but this is carefully monitored and inappropriate development is not allowed. Education is important and the national parks have 131 visitor centres and 35 environmental educational centres.

Reserves tend to be smaller and usually exist to protect a particular species or a threatened landscape. RAMSAR wetlands are wetland areas of worldwide importance and include saltmarshes, estuaries and bogs. (Ramsar was the Turkish town where the idea of international protection for wetlands was first put forward at a conference.)

PROTECTED AREAS IN ITALY, 2006

National parks	*21
National reserves	146
Regional parks	127
Regional reserves	365
RAMSAR wetlands	46
Marine protected areas	23

*(3 more currently being established)

Capo Rizzuto Marine Reserve is a 36-km stretch of coastline along the 'toe' of Italy, in the region of Calabria. It consists of eight headlands in front of which are a series of marine terraces covered with rare plant and animal communities. There are small reefs and areas covered with seaweeds known as 'submerged prairies'. Here there are sponges, a wide variety of fish and dolphins. No fishing or watersports are allowed to take place in the immediate area. Visitors can snorkel or travel in glass-bottomed boats to see the rich biodiversity of these waters. Nearby there is an aquarium, which contains specimens of the species found in the reserve.

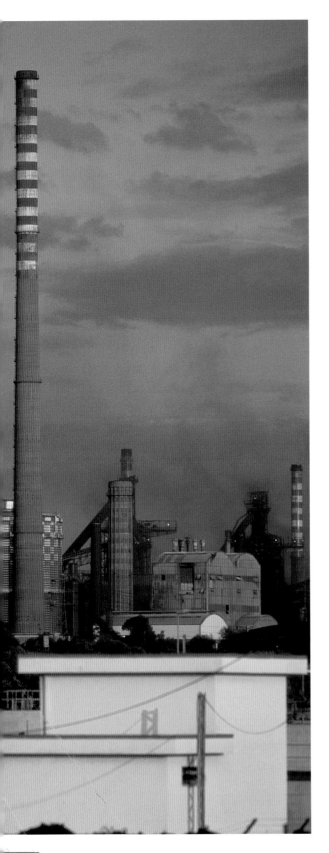

ENVIRONMENTAL PROBLEMS

Italians have become much more environmentally aware over the last decade. Air pollution has become more noticeable both in the quality of the air breathed and also in the impact it is having on Italy's buildings. Ancient architecture that has survived for hundreds of years is now being eaten away by the chemicals in the air and dissolved in the acid rain. Nearly two-thirds of Italians are more worried about air pollution than any other environmental concern,

Italian cities frequently suffer from smog caused by industrial fumes and vehicle exhaust gases.

IMPACTS OF ACID RAIN ON ITALY'S ALPINE FORESTS

The forests in the Italian Alps have also been badly affected by acid rain. Some of the effects are listed below:

- trees have yellowing leaves and more leaves drop

- damage reduces the trees' resistance to disease and pests

- trees are more prone to being blown down because they are not healthy

- if soil is very acidic, seedlings will not be able to establish

- if large numbers of trees die, soil erosion occurs because slopes are exposed to the full force of the rain

- with fewer trees, these areas are more prone to avalanches in winter.

CASE STUDY
AIR AND WATER POLLUTION IN MILAN

In an effort to reduce the levels of pollution in the city centre, Milan is one of the first Italian cities to invest in a tram system.

Milan's numerous factories and power stations contribute to large amounts of pollution in the form of gases and particulates. The Po Plain has a great deal of fog and still air, so the pollution is not easily blown away but hangs above the cities for days. Milan has run 'Car-free Sundays' quite regularly since 1999 to try to reduce the pollution. Sometimes a lack of rain can make the pollution worse as it remains in the atmosphere, causing problems for asthma and bronchitis sufferers. At the beginning of 2002, the problem was so bad that Milan had to close the city centre to cars for three days a week to clear the air.

Milan has invested in more trams and buses and has an electric car-sharing scheme. Drivers pay a membership fee and then use a magnetic card to access one of the electric cars at a number of locations. They pay for the distance travelled and return the car to another return point. There are 500 of these electric cars, helping to reduce pollution in the city centre.

There are also problems with the treatment of waste water and sewage. Even though Milan has a population of nearly 3 million, all of its sewage goes untreated into the River Lambro, a tributary of the Po. This has caused problems of eutrophication at the Po Delta.

perhaps because it is the one that affects most of them on a daily basis.

As part of the EU, Italy has signed the Kyoto Agreement, which states that the country will reduce its greenhouse gas emissions by 2008–2012 to 8 per cent lower than the figure in 1990. By 2003, Italy had in fact increased its emissions of these gases! Part of the problem is the Italians' love of cars, as well as the fact that most of Italy's electricity still comes from the burning of fossil fuels. Legambiente, Italy's most important environmental group, is campaigning for a more sustainable way of life for the country and there are branches in most large cities and towns.

CASE STUDY
ACID RAIN IN THE NORTH

Many of the industries and power stations of northern Italy produce sulphur dioxide, which can make rainfall much more acidic than normal. Added to Italy's own emissions, it receives pollutants in the winds from Germany, the Czech Republic and Slovakia. This has caused acidification of the lakes in the sub-alpine region such as Lake Como and many of its lake organisms have been greatly reduced in number. The forests in the Italian Alps have also been badly affected.

The more tourists there are, the more litter they bring with them, adding to mess on the streets.

TOURISM AND THE ENVIRONMENT

Tourism is causing problems in places such as Florence and Venice, where numbers of visitors are very high. Skiing in the winter months is also creating problems in the alpine environment. The Italian Alps are an increasingly popular ski destination but if the problems this tourism causes are not solved, Italy may well lose visitors as the environment is degraded. Mountain forests are cleared to make way for ski runs and tree-felling results in reduced avalanche control, as well as making the areas less scenic. Mountains are scarred by the installation of ski lifts.

HUNTING

Hunting is popular in Italy and most of it is carried out legally. However, one sector that is often illegal is the hunting and trapping of birds. In the north, around Lake Garda, songbirds and swallows are caught. Fine nylon nets called 'mist nets' or spring traps are used, and the birds die a slow death. A survey carried out in 2000 found that 2,000 songbirds were trapped in the area, 80 per cent of which were robins. Swallows are now protected, and several 'farms for swallows' have been set up in Italy. One was opened in

2002 on a dairy farm in the Ticino Regional Park, near Milan, where the farmer uses fewer pesticides in his farming to encourage insects and therefore attract the swallows. The farm is used as an educational resource and a recreational area for people who wish to watch the birds.

HUNTING BIRDS OF PREY

Birds of prey such as the honey buzzard migrate to Europe from Africa and use the Straits of Messina, between Sicily and the mainland, as a route to Europe. Every year hunters wait to shoot them, and until recently 5,000 protected birds of prey were illegally shot each year. Increasing awareness of their importance and careful monitoring of the Straits has meant that only a few hundred are now killed.

CASE STUDY
VENICE – A WATERY CITY

Venice was founded over 2,000 years ago and is built on wooden pilings sunk into the waters of a lagoon on the Adriatic coast. It became one of the powerful city states in the Middle Ages and attracted artists and architects, whose works are now visited by millions of tourists each year. Flooding is becoming a growing problem for the city. Water is taken from an aquifer (a rock that holds water) beneath the city and this is causing the lagoon bed to sink – 23cm over the last 100 years. Global warming is leading to an overall rise in sea levels, and there are more severe storms and tidal surges. Part of the main lagoon has had a deep channel dredged, which allows large tankers to access the industrial port area. Wash from all the ships adds to the problem of water damage, and the building of concrete quays means that there is no open land to absorb any excess water, so the city continues to flood. In 2001, St Mark's Square flooded more than 90 times.

The solution is a controversial tidal barrier in 79 hinged moving sections, which will rise from the bed of the lagoon to protect the city whenever a really high tide is predicted. The scheme is called Project Moses. Environmentalists feel that what is needed is a more sustainable scheme, including stopping the extraction of water from under the city, preventing further building around the lagoon and filling in the deep water channel, allowing only smaller vessels into the port. They argue that Venice is unique and should be preserved at all costs.

These buildings in Venice have been damaged by rising water levels. The problem is getting worse as the city suffers more frequent floods.

CHALLENGES FOR THE FUTURE

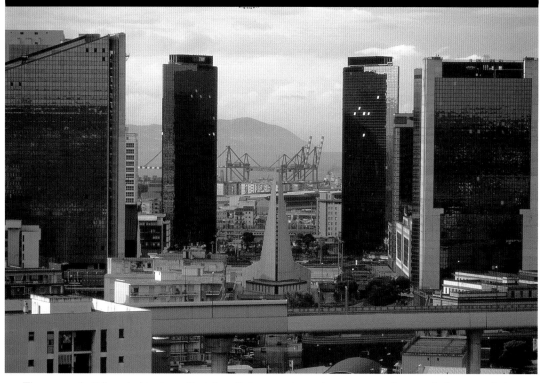

These new buildings in Naples reflect the city's move towards a more modern, varied economic base.

I taly has the eighth-strongest economy in the world, but can it maintain this? The 1992 Rio Earth Summit urged all nations to try to develop sustainable lifestyles. Italy has several problems to face in the twenty-first century, and decisions made in the next few years will impact on people and ecosystems for many years to come.

This polluted river in Lazio shows the impact of pouring waste into watercourses without proper treatment.

AGRICULTURE

Centuries of soil erosion, deforestation and overgrazing have led to poor farming landscapes. More money needs to be invested in keeping hill farmers on the land and to encourage young farmers to stay. Money needs to be made available to allow them to farm in a more environmentally friendly way, which will help preserve the traditional landscapes and yet support wildlife.

ENERGY RESOURCES

Italy is heavily dependent on the car and there are severe problems of air pollution in all its major cities because of this. Keeping to the Kyoto agreement will mean that the country must reduce its greenhouse gas emissions. That can only be done by reducing the use of fossil fuels for both transport and electricity generation. The trams in Milan and Rome and the development of green transport policies in Palermo in Sicily show the way forward. More money is being invested in alternative energy sources, but Italy's emissions are still too high to meet the targets set by the Kyoto Agreement.

THE GREYING POPULATION

Italy has an ageing population that will present serious challenges over the next 20–30 years. More services directed at the elderly must be set up, particularly because the tradition of caring for elderly parents at home may well break down under the pressures of modern living, with more women going out to work.

TOURISM

The Italians are learning to treasure their past and are beginning to move towards making tourists pay a price that includes cover for the damage they cause just by being there. This is not only direct damage but includes their contribution to pollution in a city by using a car or having arrived by air, having an impact on greenhouse gases. In Florence, although fewer tourists are allowed into the Ufizzi (see page 49) there has not been a reduction in revenues and the collection is not put under as much strain.

MIGRATION

This may turn from a problem at the beginning of the twenty-first century into a blessing later on as there are not enough young people working in Italy to support the growing population of elderly people or to fill the jobs of the future. Italy needs help from

Pensioners enjoying the sun. Italy's huge pension bill must be reduced, so younger people will have to work for longer than their parents to have a pension.

the EU to police its extensive coastal boundaries so that international migrants who wish to live in Italy do so legally and can be given suitable support to begin a new life.

BRIDGING THE DIVIDE

Italy as a young nation came into its own during the twentieth century and now wishes to continue to be able to sustain its lifestyle well into the twenty-first. There is a need to develop the south of the country so that there is less of a divide between the northern and southern regions. There are forces in the north that want to become independent from the southern region, which they regard as a drain on their economy. That may be the greatest challenge for the future; ensuring that the south continues to develop and be a full partner within the country of Italy.

GLOSSARY

Acid rain Rainfall that is more acid than usual, caused by rainwater mixing with pollutants such as sulphur dioxide and nitrous oxides.

Agribusiness Commercial farming on a large scale. It is highly mechanised and dependent on chemicals, and is often owned by finance companies.

Alpine tundra A vegetation zone found high up mountains, beyond the treeline. Most of the vegetation includes mosses, lichens and low growing grasses.

Altitude The measurement of height above sea level.

Aqueduct An artificial channel constructed to carry water.

Biodiversity The variety of species found within an area.

Coalition A grouping together of several organisations or political parties who then act as one.

Counterurbanisation The movement of people away from urban centres to smaller villages and towns.

Deforestation Cutting down trees and not replanting them.

Delta A triangular-shaped landscape feature made up of sediments transported by a river and deposited at its mouth.

Desertification Creation of desert-like conditions in arid areas, usually by human actions, such as over-grazing and deforestation.

Diversification The expansion of a company's or an economy's activities in order to make more profit.

Emigrant A person who leaves a country or region to live elsewhere.

European Union (EU) A group of countries that are working together financially, economically and socially.

Eutrophication The enrichment of fresh water by excess nutrients. This results in huge amounts of algae growing. When they die and decay most of the oxygen in the water is used up and very little can live in it.

Flagship store An important shop, usually found in capital and major cities, where all the latest merchandise and marketing technology is used to highlight the company concerned.

Floodplain The wide floor of a river valley over which it may flood.

Fold mountains Mountains created by pressure within the Earth's crust, which causes layers of rock to slowly fold in on themselves and rise up.

Fossil fuel Fuels including coal, oil and gas made up of the fossilised remains of plants and micro-organisms that lived millions of years ago.

GDP (Gross Domestic Product) The total monetary value of goods and services produced by a country in a single year.

Geothermal energy Energy extracted from water or steam heated by hot rocks below the Earth's surface.

Glacier A slow-moving river of ice found mainly in high mountains.

GNI (Gross National Income) Sometimes called the Gross National Product, or GNP, this is the total value of goods and services produced by a country, plus any earnings from overseas, in a single year.

High-tech industry Industry that uses the latest production techniques and technology such as computing and electronics.

Immigrant A person who comes to live in a new country or region.

Intensive agriculture Agriculture with high inputs of labour or fertilisers over a small area.

Levee A raised bank that is formed naturally by a river, although humans may build them up higher as a form of flood protection.

Multi-purpose forestry Forestry that provides space for recreation, conservation and education, as well as extracting timber.

Peninsula Land surrounded on three sides by water.

Photovoltaic cells Cells that can produce electrical power when sunlight falls on them.

Plain A large area of flat land.

Plate A very large section of the Earth's crust composed of rock several kilometres thick, which moves slowly across the planet's surface.

Richter scale A measurement used to determine the size of an earthquake.

Salinisation The accumulation of salt in the soil, often as a result of excessive irrigation.

Service industry An industry that provides services to the public, such as transportation, communications and tourism.

Soil erosion The wearing away and transportation of the soil layer.

Surface run-off The overland movement of water after rainfall.

Teleworking Working from home for a company by using the Internet via a phone line.

Transnational company (TNC) A large company that trades globally and with factories in several countries.

Tributary A river that joins a larger river.

Watershed The boundary of a drainage basin.

United Nations (UN) An international peace-keeping organisation.

FURTHER INFORMATION

BOOKS TO READ:

NON-FICTION:

Changing Face of Italy by Kathryn Britton (Hodder Wayland, 2002) Illustrated reference for KS2–3.

Eyewitness Travel Guide to Italy (Dorling Kindersley, 2003) A travel guide with lots of maps, cut-away drawings of buildings and excellent photographs of Italy.

Rough Guide to Italy by Ros Belford (Rough Guides, 2003) A travel guide containing lots of information, maps and photographs of Italy.

Ripe for the Picking by Annie Haws (Penguin, 2003) A lively and entertaining account of an Englishwoman's life in Liguria.

FICTION:

Daughter of Venice by Donna Jo Napoli (Wendy Lamb Books, 2002) The story of a young noble girl in sixteenth-century Venice, just after the Renaissance period.

WEBSITES:

GENERAL INFORMATION:
CIA World Factbook
www.cia.gov/cia/publications/factbook/geos/it.html
Lots of up to date information on Italy.

Italian Embassy website
www.embitaly.org.uk
Information on history, the regions and the cities of Italy.

NATIONAL PARKS:
www.parks.it/indice/NatParks.html
This website provides lots of information, photos and links to Italian national parks.

EUROPEAN UNION:
Europa
www.europa.eu.int/
A website that has links to institutions, information, the latest news and an excellent statistics section.

TOURIST INFORMATION:
Italian Tourist Board
www.enit.it/default.asp?Lang=UK
An information site for nature, history, art and tours within Italy.

RIVER PO:
River Po Basin Authority
www.adbpo.it/inglese/testouk.html
Provides information on the management of Italy's longest river and its tributaries.

A market trader sets out his stall in Palermo.

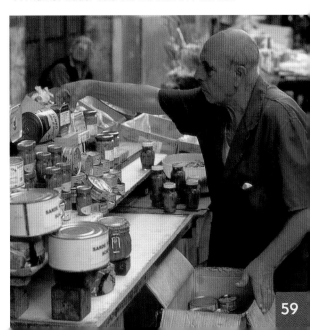

INDEX

Numbers shown in **bold** refer to pages with maps, graphic illustrations or photographs.

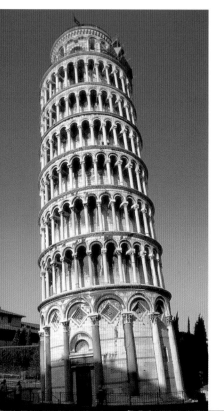

The leaning tower of Pisa is one of Italy's most famous tourist attractions.

Tourists enjoy a trip on a gondola in Venice.